CURRICULUM MATERIALS
CENTER

YO-EHZ-511

*elem
R
Z 65
R443
L 574
1999
m

3-200

HYMNS OF THE FAITHFUL SERIES

LENT EASTER

WRITTEN BY

Richard Resch

PROPERTY OF
CONCORDIA COLLEGE LIBRARY
BRONXVILLE, NEW YORK 10708

CPH.
Concordia Publishing House

Series editor: Thomas J. Doyle

This publication is available in braille and in large print for the visually impaired. Write to the Library for the Blind, 1333 S. Kirkwood Rd., St. Louis, MO 63122-7295; or call 1-800-433-3954.

All Scripture quotations are from the HOLY BIBLE, NEW INTERNATIONAL VERSION®. NIV®. Copyright © 1973, 1978, 1984 by International Bible Society. Used by permission of Zondervan Publishing House. All rights reserved.

Copyright © 1999 Concordia Publishing House
3558 S. Jefferson Avenue, St. Louis, MO 63118-3968
Manufactured in the United States of America

All rights reserved. No part of this publication may be reproduced, stored in a retrieval system, or transmitted, in any form or by any means, electronic, mechanical, photocopying, recording, or otherwise, without the prior written permission of Concordia Publishing House.

1 2 3 4 5 6 7 8 9 10   08 07 06 05 04 03 02 01 00 99

Contents

All Glory, Laud, and Honor

Focus

Many countries have at least one national hero. Other countries may have many national heroes.

1. List the names of some national heroes. Next to each name write the reason that person became a national hero.

2. What events occurred or are occurring to celebrate and give honor to these national heroes?

Inform

Sing "All Glory, Laud, and Honor" (*LW* 102).

Refrain: *All glory, laud, and honor*
To You, Redeemer, King,
To whom the lips of children
Made sweet hosannas ring.

1. *You are the king of Israel*
And David's royal Son,
Now in the Lord's name coming,
Our King and Blessed One.
Refrain

2. *The company of angels*
Are praising You on high;
Creation and all mortals
In chorus make reply.
Refrain

3. *The multitude of pilgrims*
With palms before You went,
Our praise and prayer and anthems
Before You we present.
Refrain

4. *To You, before Your Passion,*
They sang their hymns of praise.
To You, now high exalted,
Our melody we raise.
Refrain

5. *Their praises You accepted;*
Accept the prayers we bring,
Great author of all goodness,
O good and gracious King.
Refrain

Read Matthew 21:1–11.

1. How well do the words and melody of the hymn capture the Palm Sunday event recorded in Scripture? Explain.

2. Jesus rides into Jerusalem as a hero. What glory does the crowd hope Jesus will accomplish? How is this glory different than the glory Jesus will experience? See Matthew 27:32–46.

3. Jesus proclaims victory for us over sin, death, and the power of the devil when He rises from the grave. What glory did Jesus win for us through His death on the cross (1 Peter 5:10)?

Connect

1. What do you confess in this hymn?

2. How is Jesus a hero for you? What makes His heroic actions on your behalf greater than any other hero's actions?

3. How can we glorify (give glory to) Jesus, who by His death provides us glory?

Vision

Consider this week opportunities you have to demonstrate the refrain of this hymn in what you say and what you do.

All glory, laud, and honor
To You, Redeemer, King,
To whom the lips of children
Made sweet hosannas ring.

All Glory, Laud, and Honor

Theodulf of Orléans, 750/760–821
Tr. John M. Neale, 1818–66, alt.

VALET WILL ICH DIR GEBEN
Melchior Teschner, 1584–1635

Refrain: All glo - ry, laud, and hon - or To You, Re - deem - er, King, To whom the lips of chil - dren Made sweet ho - san - nas ring.

1 You are the king of Is - rael And Da - vid's roy - al Son, Now in the Lord's name com - ing, Our King and Bless - ed One.
2 The com - pa - ny of an - gels Are prais - ing You on high; Cre - a - tion and all mor - tals In cho - rus make re - ply.
3 The mul - ti - tude of pil - grims With palms be - fore You went, Our praise and prayer and an - thems Be - fore You we pre - sent.
4 To You, be - fore Your Pas - sion, They sang their hymns of praise. To You, now high ex - alt - ed, Our mel - o - dy we raise.

Refrain

5 Their praises You accepted, Accept the prayers we bring,
Great author of all goodness, O good and gracious King. *Refrain*

Study Sheet 2
Glory Be to Jesus

Focus

1. For what kind of behavior are we most apt to praise someone?

2. For what behavior are we most likely to withhold praise?

Inform

Sing together "Glory Be to Jesus" (LW 98).

1. *Glory be to Jesus,*
   Who in bitter pains
   Poured for me the lifeblood
   From His sacred veins.

2. *Grace and life eternal*
   In that blood I find;
   Blest be His compassion,
   Infinitely kind.

3. *Blest through endless ages*
   Be the precious stream
   Which from endless torment
   Did the world redeem.

4. *Abel's blood for vengeance*
   Pleaded to the skies;
   But the blood of Jesus
   For our pardon cries.

5. *Oft as earth exulting*
   Wafts its praise on high,
   Angel hosts rejoicing
   Make their glad reply.

6. *Lift we then our voices,*
   Swell the mighty flood;
   Louder still and louder
   Praise the precious blood.

1. Read 1 Peter 1:18–21 and Hebrews 9:11–14. How well do the hymn stanzas capture the truth revealed in Scripture? Give the reason for your answer.

2. For what do we praise Jesus in the sixth stanza?

3. How is the portrait of glory painted in the hymn different than the typical human understanding of glory?

Connect

1. Unlike "All Glory, Laud, and Honor," this hymn doesn't appear in all of the present hymnals of Christendom. In fact, some hymnals exclude this hymn because of its gruesome nature. In your opinion, is it appropriate or inappropriate to focus on the gruesome nature of crucifixion? Do you think this hymn should or should not be included in a hymnal? Why?

2. What glory do you receive because of the glory of the cross?

3. Recall the behaviors for which we would give or withhold praise. Is it appropriate for us to praise Jesus for His behavior—suffering and dying on the cross? Why or why not?

Vision

In the coming week, memorize one stanza of the hymn each day. During the day, meditate on the words of the stanza you are memorizing. Praise and thank God for the shed blood of His own dear Son. Jesus has washed you in His blood. Your sins are forgiven.

Glory Be to Jesus

Italian, 18th cent.
Tr. Edward Caswall, 1814–78

WEM IN LEIDENSTAGEN
Friedrich Filitz, 1804–76

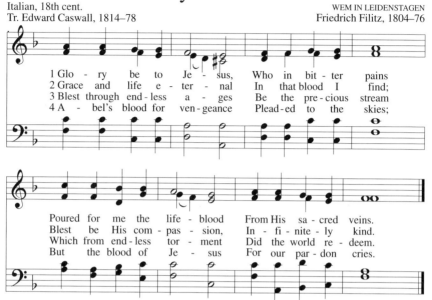

1 Glo - ry be to Je - sus, Who in bit - ter pains
2 Grace and life e - ter - nal In that blood I find;
3 Blest through end - less a - ges Be the pre - cious stream
4 A - bel's blood for ven - geance Plead - ed to the skies;

Poured for me the life - blood From His sa - cred veins.
Blest be His com - pas - sion, In - fi - nite - ly kind.
Which from end - less tor - ment Did the world re - deem.
But the blood of Je - sus For our par - don cries.

5 Oft as earth exulting
  Wafts its praise on high,
Angel hosts rejoicing
  Make their glad reply.

6 Lift we then our voices,
  Swell the mighty flood;
Louder still and louder
  Praise the precious blood.

O Sacred Head, Now Wounded

Focus

1. What type of events might cause us to "look the other way"?

2. Why might we look the other way when witnessing an unpleasant event?

Inform

Sing together "O Sacred Head, Now Wounded" (*LW* 113).

1. O sacred head, now wounded,
   With grief and shame weighed down,
   Now scornfully surrounded
   With thorns, Your only crown.
   O sacred head, what glory
   And bliss did once combine;
   Though now despised and gory,
   I joy to call You mine!

2. How pale You are with anguish,
   With sore abuse and scorn!
   Your face, Your eyes now languish,
   Which once were bright as morn.
   Now from Your cheeks has vanished
   Their color once so fair;
   From loving lips is banished
   The splendor that was there.

3. All this for my transgression,
   My wayward soul to win;
   This torment of Your Passion,
   To set me free from sin.
   I cast myself before You,
   Your wrath my rightful lot;
   Have mercy, I implore You,
   O Lord, condemn me not!

4. Here will I stand beside You,
   Your death for me my plea;
   Let all the world deride You,
   I clasp You close to me.
   My awe cannot be spoken,
   To see You crucified;
   But in Your body broken,
   Redeemed, I safely hide!

5. What language can I borrow
   To thank You, dearest friend,
   For this Your dying sorrow,
   Your mercy without end?
   Bind me to You forever,
   Give courage from above;
   Let not my weakness sever
   Your bond of lasting love.

6. Lord, be my consolation,
   My constant source of cheer;
   Remind me of Your Passion,
   My shield when death is near.
   I look in faith, believing
   That You have died for me;
   Your cross and crown receiving,
   I live eternally.

1. Read the following Scripture references: Psalm 22:6–8; Isaiah 50:6; Matthew 27:28–31; and John 19:1–6. Write the Scripture references next to the similar words found in the hymn.

2. Describe the emotion captured by the hymn writer.

3. This hymn in recent years has become less and less popular. Consider people's attitude toward sin today. How might people's attitude toward sin be a cause of the hymn's decreasing popularity?

4. Why is it important for the church to proclaim the brutality of the cross?

Connect

1. Why might the words of the hymn cause us to turn away?

2. Underline the words or phrases from the hymn that are most meaningful to you. Explain the reason for your choice.

Vision

Every day this week, speak the words of the hymn in prayer. On the first day speak stanza 1. On the second day speak stanzas 1 and 2. On the third day speak stanzas 1, 2, and 3. As you continue in this pattern, consider the pain and anguish Jesus endured because of our sin.

O Sacred Head, Now Wounded

Attr. Bernard of Clairvaux, 1091–1153
Paul Gerhardt, 1607–76; tr. *Lutheran Worship*, 1982

HERZLICH TUT MICH VERLANGEN
Hans L. Hassler, 1564–1612

1 O sa-cred head, now wound-ed, With grief and shame weighed down,
2 How pale You are with an-guish, With sore a-buse and scorn!
3 All this for my trans-gres-sion, My way-ward soul to win;
4 Here will I stand be-side You, Your death for me my plea;

Now scorn-ful-ly sur-round-ed With thorns, Your on-ly crown.
Your face, Your eyes now lan-guish, Which once were bright as morn.
This tor-ment of Your Pas-sion, To set me free from sin.
Let all the world de-ride You, I clasp You close to me.

O sa-cred head, what glo-ry And bliss did once com-bine;
Now from Your cheeks has van-ished Their col-or once so fair;
I cast my-self be-fore You, Your wrath my right-ful lot;
My awe can-not be spo-ken, To see You cru-ci-fied;

Though now de-spised and gor-y, I joy to call You mine!
From lov-ing lips is ban-ished The splen-dor that was there.
Have mer-cy, I im-plore You, O Lord, con-demn me not!
But in Your bod-y bro-ken, Re-deemed, I safe-ly hide!

5 What language can I borrow
   To thank You, dearest friend,
For this Your dying sorrow,
   Your mercy without end?
Bind me to You forever,
   Give courage from above;
Let not my weakness sever
   Your bond of lasting love.

6 Lord, be my consolation,
   My constant source of cheer;
Remind me of Your Passion,
   My shield when death is near.
I look in faith, believing
   That You have died for me;
Your cross and crown receiving,
   I live eternally.

Go to Dark Gethsemane

Focus

1. When receiving a gift a person might exclaim, "For me!?" What might cause a person to speak these words?

2. When considering Jesus' death on the cross, why might a person exclaim, "For me!?"?

Inform

Sing together "Go to Dark Gethsemane" (*LW* 110).

1. *Go to dark Gethsemane,*
    All who feel the tempter's pow'r;
    Your Redeemer's conflict see.
    Watch with Him one bitter hour;
    Turn not from His griefs away;
    Learn from Jesus Christ to pray.

2. *Follow to the judgment hall,*
    View the Lord of life arraigned;
    Oh, the wormwood and the gall!
    Oh, the pangs His soul sustained!
    Shun not suff'ring, shame, or loss;
    Learn from Him to bear the cross.

3. *Calv'ry's mournful mountain climb;*
    There, adoring at His feet,
    Mark that miracle of time,
    God's own sacrifice complete.
    "It is finished!" hear Him cry;
    Learn from Jesus Christ to die.

4. *Early hasten to the tomb*
    Where they laid His breathless clay;
    All is solitude and gloom.
    Who has taken Him away?
    Christ is ris'n! He meets our eyes.
    Savior, teach us so to rise.

1. Read Matthew 26:36–46 and Luke 24:17–32. How well does the hymn capture the essence of these Scripture passages?

2. Some have described "Go to Dark Gethsemane" as a hymn of movement. Why might it be considered such?

3. Review the Lenten hymns studied so far. What makes this hymn unique? Hint: See stanza 4. Is it appropriate for a Lenten hymn to include a stanza concerning the resurrection? Why or why not?

Connect

1. Why is it important to remember that Jesus endured the cross "for me"?

2. What might lead us to ask, "For me?" when considering the magnitude of God's love in Jesus as it's described in the words of the hymn?

Vision

Consider taking the journey once again to Gethsemane with Jesus by studying the different Gospel accounts of the passion this week. Pray that the Holy Spirit would provide you an opportunity to take along a friend or loved one as you "Go to Dark Gethsemane."

Go to Dark Gethsemane

James Montgomery, 1771–1854

GETHSEMANE
Richard Redhead, 1820–1901

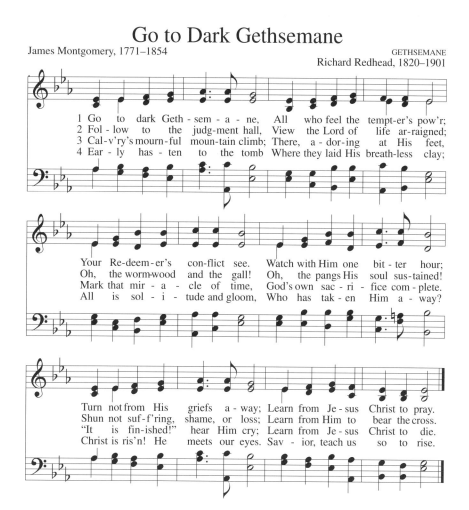

1 Go to dark Geth - sem - a - ne, All who feel the tempt-er's pow'r;
2 Fol - low to the judg-ment hall, View the Lord of life ar-raigned;
3 Cal-v'ry's mourn-ful moun-tain climb; There, a - dor-ing at His feet,
4 Ear - ly has - ten to the tomb Where they laid His breath-less clay;

Your Re-deem-er's con-flict see. Watch with Him one bit - ter hour;
Oh, the worm-wood and the gall! Oh, the pangs His soul sus-tained!
Mark that mir - a - cle of time, God's own sac - ri - fice com - plete.
All is sol - i - tude and gloom, Who has tak - en Him a - way?

Turn not from His griefs a - way; Learn from Je - sus Christ to pray.
Shun not suf-f'ring, shame, or loss; Learn from Him to bear the cross.
"It is fin-ished!" hear Him cry; Learn from Je - sus Christ to die.
Christ is ris'n! He meets our eyes. Sav - ior, teach us so to rise.

PROPERTY OF
CONCORDIA COLLEGE LIBRARY
BRONXVILLE, NEW YORK 10708

15

I Know That My Redeemer Lives

Focus

1. List all of the words that come to mind when you think of a funeral.

2. Now group the words that seem to go together.

3. Next label the groups of words with a one-word description.

4. Now create a one- or two-sentence description of a funeral, using the labels with which you described each group.

5. Consider your written description of a funeral as you sing "I Know That My Redeemer Lives."

Inform

Sing "I Know That My Redeemer Lives" (*LW* 264).

1. I know that my Redeemer lives!
   What comfort this sweet sentence gives!
   He lives, He lives, who once was dead;
   He lives, my ever-living head!

2. He lives triumphant from the grave;
   He lives eternally to save;
   He lives exalted, throned above;
   He lives to rule His Church in love.

3. He lives to grant me rich supply;
   He lives to guide me with His eye;
   He lives to comfort me when faint;
   He lives to hear my soul's complaint.

4. He lives to silence all my fears;
   He lives to wipe away my tears;
   He lives to calm my troubled heart;
   He lives all blessings to impart.

5. He lives to bless me with His love;
   He lives to plead for me above;
   He lives my hungry soul to feed;
   He lives to help in time of need.

6. He lives, my kind, wise, heav'nly friend;
   He lives and loves me to the end;
   He lives, and while He lives, I'll sing;
   He lives, my Prophet, Priest, and King!

7. He lives and grants me daily breath;
   He lives, and I shall conquer death;
   He lives my mansion to prepare;
   He lives to bring me safely there.

8. He lives, all glory to His name!
   He lives, my Savior, still the same;
   What joy this blest assurance gives:
   I know that my Redeemer lives!

Read Job 19:25–27; John 14:2–4; and Hebrews 7:23–25.

1. The words of this familiar hymn come from a number of portions of Scripture. What do each of the Scripture references have in common!

2. How well has the author of "I Know That My Redeemer Lives" captured the truth found in Scripture concerning life and death?

3. Often hymnals are divided into topical sections. In some hymnals this hymn is found in the section labeled "Easter," in others "Death and Burial," and in others "Christian Hope." Review the words of the hymn and then tell why it is appropriately positioned under each of these sections.

4. Now, read through the words of several Easter hymns. How many of them speak about human death? Why is it appropriate to consider death on Easter, the day we celebrate life?

Connect

1. How would you describe the message of this hymn in one or two sentences?

2. What words of this hymn would provide comfort to you as face your own death?

3. What words of this hymn would provide comfort to those who grieve the loss of a loved one?

4. Why do many consider this hymn a bold confession of faith? How might you use the words of this hymn to confess your faith in the crucified and risen Jesus?

Vision

1. Meditate on the words of "I Know That My Redeemer Lives" this week. Give thanks to God for that which He has accomplished for you in the person and work of Jesus.

2. Each day this week, study a different Easter hymn. Consider the message in each hymn. What does the message mean for your life? for your death?

3. Share with a friend or loved one the hope and comfort you have in confessing, "I know that my Redeemer lives!"

I Know That My Redeemer Lives

Samuel Medley, 1738–99, alt.

DUKE STREET
Attr. John Hatton, d. 1793

1 I know that my Re - deem - er lives! What com-fort
2 He lives tri - um - phant from the grave; He lives e -
3 He lives to grant me rich sup - ply; He lives to
4 He lives to si - lence all my fears; He lives to

this sweet sen - tence gives! He lives, He lives, who
ter - nal - ly to save; He lives ex - alt - ed,
guide me with His eye; He lives to com - fort
wipe a - way my tears; He lives to calm my

once was dead; He lives, my ev - er - liv - ing head!
throned a - bove; He lives to rule His Church in love.
me when faint; He lives to hear my soul's com - plaint.
trou - bled heart; He lives all bless - ings to im - part.

5 He lives to bless me with His love;
He lives to plead for me above;
He lives my hungry soul to feed;
He lives to help in time of need.

6 He lives, my kind, wise, heav'nly friend;
He lives and loves me to the end;
He lives, and while He lives, I'll sing;
He lives, my Prophet, Priest, and King!

7 He lives and grants me daily breath;
He lives, and I shall conquer death;
He lives my mansion to prepare;
He lives to bring me safely there.

8 He lives, all glory to His name!
He lives, my Savior, still the same;
What joy this blest assurance gives:
I know that my Redeemer lives!

At the Lamb's High Feast We Sing

Focus

1. On what occasions do we often celebrate with a feast?

2. Why is a feast an appropriate way to celebrate these occasions?

3. Can you think of other occasions that would be appropriate to celebrate with a feast? Why?

Inform

Sing "At the Lamb's High Feast We Sing" (*LW* 126).

1. *At the Lamb's high feast we sing*
   Praise to our victorious king,
   Who has washed us in the tide
   Flowing from His pierced side.
   Alleluia!

2. *Praise we Him, whose love divine*
   Gives His sacred blood for wine,
   Gives His body for the feast—
   Christ the victim, Christ the priest.
   Alleluia!

3. *Where the paschal blood is poured,*
   Death's dread angel sheathes the sword;
   Israel's hosts triumphant go
   Through the wave that drowns the foe.
   Alleluia!

4. *Praise we Christ, whose blood was shed,*
   Paschal victim, paschal bread;
   With sincerity and love
   Eat we manna from above.
   Alleluia!

5. *Mighty Victim from the sky,*
   Hell's fierce pow'rs beneath You lie;
   You have conquered in the fight,
   You have brought us life and light.
   Alleluia!

6. *Now no more can death appall,*
   Now no more the grave enthrall;
   You have opened paradise,
   And Your saints in You shall rise.
   Alleluia!

7. *Easter triumph, Easter joy!*
   This alone can sin destroy;
   From sin's pow'r, Lord, set us free,
   Newborn souls in You to be.
   Alleluia!

8. *Father, who the crown shall give,*
   Savior, by whose death we live,
   Spirit, guide through all our days:
   Three in One, Your name we praise.
   Alleluia!

Read the biblical sources from which the text of this hymn came: Exodus 12:21–23; 14:22; Matthew 26:26–29; 1 Corinthians 5:6–8; and Revelation 5:11–13.

1. Consider the textual sources of this hymn. How do the stanzas of the hymn tie so many different sources together in a unified theme?

2. This hymn, like many other Latin hymns, concludes with a doxology—praise to Father, Son, and Holy Spirit. Why is this ending fitting to the message proclaimed in the preceding stanzas? Consider: Ambrose (340–97), Bishop of Milan, used hymns to battle the Arian controversy, a heresy that attacked the trinitarian nature of God.

3. This hymn develops three striking images of Jesus Christ: the Host who provides the sacrifice; the Priest who offers the sacrifice; and the Victim who is the sacrifice. How is each of these three images appropriate in describing the person and work of Jesus on our behalf?

4. This hymn is found in a number of topical sections in different hymnals: "Lord's Supper," "Maundy Thursday," and "Easter." In which section do you believe this hymn most appropriately belongs? Why?

5. Comment on the following quote by F. Samuel Janzow, one of the text editors of *Lutheran Worship*, concerning this hymn:

> *The Easter joy of faith's feeding upon Christ and His sin-and-death-and-hell-conquering crucifixion and resurrection is poetically pictured in this hymn as a feast at which the blood of the Lamb is the wine which faith drinks, and the Lamb's flesh, or body, is the food upon which it feeds during this victory banquet.*

How is the Lord's Supper a victory banquet?

Connect

1. How does the feast described in this hymn affect you and your life?

2. Each stanza of the hymn ends with "Alleluia!" Why does the blood shed by Jesus on the cross give you reason to shout "Alleluia!"? Why does the resurrection give you reason to shout "Alleluia!"? Why does the celebration of the Lord's Supper give you reason to shout "Alleluia!"?

3. How do the events described in this hymn give you reason to celebrate with a feast?

Vision

1. Meditate on each of the stanzas of the hymn this week.

2. Give thanks and praise to the Lamb, who was slain so that the sheep who have gone astray might be united with the Shepherd into eternity.

3. Share with a friend or loved one the feast of victory won for you by Jesus on the cross and proclaimed in His resurrection from the dead.

At the Lamb's High Feast We Sing

Office Hymn, 17th cent.
Tr. Robert Campbell, 1814–68, alt.

SONNE DER GERECHTIGKEIT
Bohemian Brethren, *Kirchengeseng*, 1566

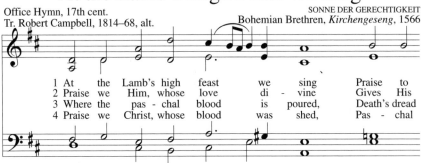

1 At the Lamb's high feast we sing Praise to
2 Praise we Him, whose love di - vine Gives His
3 Where the pas - chal blood is poured, Death's dread
4 Praise we Christ, whose blood was shed, Pas - chal

our vic - to - rious king, Who has washed us
sa - cred blood for wine, Gives His bod - y
an - gel sheathes the sword; Is - rael's hosts tri-
vic - tim, pas - chal bread; With sin - cer - i-

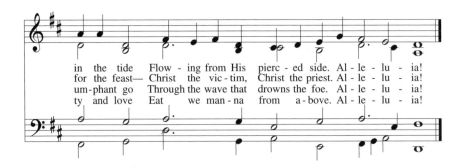

in the tide Flow - ing from His pierc - ed side. Al - le - lu - ia!
for the feast— Christ the vic - tim, Christ the priest. Al - le - lu - ia!
um-phant go Through the wave that drowns the foe. Al - le - lu - ia!
ty and love Eat we man - na from a - bove. Al - le - lu - ia!

5 Mighty Victim from the sky,
Hell's fierce pow'rs beneath You lie;
You have conquered in the fight,
You have brought us life and light.
Alleluia!

6 Now no more can death appall,
Now no more the grave enthrall;
You have opened paradise,
And Your saints in You shall rise.
Alleluia!

7 Easter triumph, Easter joy!
This alone can sin destroy;
From sin's pow'r, Lord, set us free,
Newborn souls in You to be.
Alleluia!

8 Father, who the crown shall give,
Savior, by whose death we live,
Spirit, guide through all our days:
Three in One, Your name we praise.
Alleluia!